CÉZANNE

THE GREAT ARTISTS COLLECTION

MASON CREST

Contents

4

2

14

26

Introduction   4

Cézanne – **A Biography**   14

Great Works – **Paintings***   26

Cézanne – **In The 21ˢᵗ Century**   62

*Great Works order is alphabetical where possible.

CÉZANNE

Mason Crest
450 Parkway Drive, Suite D
Broomall, PA 19008
www.masoncrest.com

Printed and bound in the United States of America.

10 9 8 7 6 5 4 3 2

Cataloging-in-Publication Data on file with the Library of Congress.

Series ISBN: 978-1-4222-3256-9
Hardback ISBN: 978-1-4222-3257-6
ebook ISBN: 978-1-4222-8534-3

Written by: Jessica Toyne

Images courtesy of PA Photos and Scala Archives

"Art is a harmony parallel with nature."
Paul Cézanne

Introduction

(Mary Evans Picture Library)

■ **ABOVE:** Paul Cézanne in 1890.

Paul Cézanne was highly revered by not just his contemporaries, but also the 20th- and 21st-century artists that were to follow him. Perhaps this is because his paintings and great works were universal and easy to interpret, with monumental great landscapes, seascapes, portraits, railway subjects, and portraitures, or perhaps it is because he brought something fresh, exciting, and new. (His style and techniques were much copied by new upcoming artists at the turn of the century.) Described by Henri Matisse as: "the father of us all," and also known as "Father of Modernism," Cézanne's style and influences changed, from his early "darker" palettes to colorful and vibrant pieces. The paintings from the 1870s developed through Impressionism – still widely regarded as one of the greatest movements in the art world – to his later works into the 20th century, with their foundations firmly and geometrically routed in Cubism. He lived and worked through a time when Impressionism was in its heyday, and he frequently used these techniques, but he is more often than not considered a Post-Impressionist.

(Public Domain)

■ **ABOVE:** An exterior view of the Louvre.

He was an innovator – although he didn't intend to be and was quite surprised that his works inspired the likes of Gauguin – and would often paint the same scene or subject literally hundreds of times while exploring different colors and techniques. However, he was much misunderstood at the start of his career, and despite using Impressionist techniques, he was much maligned by many of his contemporaries who felt his works were far too controversial. He was a true modernist, ahead of his time.

Cézanne was a diverse artist, slow to work and quick to admonish his own achievements, yet he tackled many difficult, complex, and painstaking projects throughout a career that spanned almost 50 years. He has been particularly influential and much celebrated during the first decade of the 21st century and beyond – and many solo exhibitions have been held – so what exactly did this extraordinary French artist achieve that has contributed to his legacy more than 100 years after his death? Many of his works, interpreted from the great masters, show that he had a considered understanding for the artists that had gone before. However, he would always add his own beliefs to the compositions he was creating. He spent many hours studying in the Louvre and made studies of individual figures, which he then adapted for his own paintings. While he certainly made his paintings his own, he didn't want to leave his audiences wondering where the inspiration came from, and it was his wish for the original works to be identified. His influences didn't just include art history, he was also interested in the contemporary art scene and the influence of color, as well as what was happening in literary circles and the beauty in nature that surrounded him. It was an eclectic mix that was to provide the foundation of some of the most complex and interesting art that was to endure. He was much admired by Gauguin, Monet, Picasso, and Munch; in fact, he had gained considerable recognition toward the later part of his career. As is commonplace, much of the artist's thoughts, ideas, and influences have come to be known through the letters he wrote, as well as the writings and conversations he had with his contemporaries.

His style and technique changed considerably, and possibly drastically, through his career, starting with the early dark works with thick paint comprised of black and earth tones, often worked with a palette knife. However, his influential mentor, Pissarro, would introduce him to a new world of color and the countryside, enthused with paintings built up with layer upon layer of color. He was also drawn to rigid horizontal, vertical, and diagonal lines, which developed into a diagonal hatching stroke that could be applied evenly from one side of the canvas

■ ABOVE: French artist Paul Gauguin who was influenced by Cézanne.

7

Claude Monet

■ **ABOVE:** Artist Claude Monet was an admirer of Cézanne's work.

to the other. This was carefully crafted and painstaking work, but it gave Cézanne's paintings a "knitting" of brushstrokes that were used to great effect across many of his pieces. The original flat brushstrokes were added to by layers of contrasting light and dark tones, which helped to give a three-dimensional effect. He was quick to realize that capturing the various stages of light, which would undoubtedly cross the canvas as he surveyed a panoramic vision, when applied to his landscapes, was virtually impossible. As he worked slowly, Cézanne chose to work indoors and not *en plein air* (outside), and so developed his own way of interpreting the light and shadows by leaving patches and streaks of the canvas bare to accentuate and "capture" the light that could not be achieved by color alone. While a large number of artists chose to work in watercolors before moving their subjects on to oils, Cézanne chose to work in watercolors as a medium in their own right, even though he often then reworked the canvas in oils. Watercolors were a much lighter medium than oils for Cézanne, who could be heavy-handed with the palette knife and the amount of oil he used. It was also a more delicate way of working for the man who was renowned for his often "aggressive" approach to his oil paintings.

Cézanne was convinced that everything that existed was made up of geometric shapes comprising the cylinder, cone, and sphere, and he focused on them in his works in a total belief that they would prove true to life. It was to give Cézanne's paintings a uniqueness that resulted in a depth not seen before, perhaps giving rise to the miscomprehension he received from his contemporaries in Paris in the early days. What upset Cézanne about Impressionism was its avoidance of realism, which to him, was extremely important. As his style developed, the flat brushstrokes that had been so carefully built on with contrasting light and dark tones made way for patches of distinct color. It was this that was to influence the Cubists, who were particularly taken with Cézanne's carefully applied colors that provided depth and perspective. The artist was a perfectionist with great attention to detail, however, he wasn't averse to treating subjects with an element of distortion, and accuracy in perspective would be overtaken in the pursuit of expression and character. Just like his paintings, with their contrasts and balance, Cézanne was a man with two sides. While he had little, or no acceptable table manners, he was renowned as a gentleman who was extremely polite and courteous. Shy and notoriously bohemian, Cézanne was surprising and contradictory. He went faithfully to church, yet despised religious authority. He was interested and respectful of

9

(Public Domain)

■ **ABOVE: A Camille Pissarro self-portrait, 1873. Pissarro was a contemporary of Cézanne's.**

(Interfoto / A. Koch / Mary Evans)

■ **ABOVE:** An unfinished landscape using watercolor and pencil.

tradition, but had no qualms in overriding it, and while he adored Paris and all that it offered him, he couldn't wait to escape to the country in order to find peace and solitude.

Perhaps Cézanne's pursuit of perfection was the cause for his ripping up canvases or working and reworking a painting hundreds of times. However, perhaps the fact that his contemporaries, Pissarro – whom he often painted alongside – Manet, Renoir, and Monet were beginning to gain recognition, while he remained unaccepted by critics and completely misunderstood by the public, is why he chose to work furiously – he had an unyielding work ethic – and remain in isolation. He wanted a depth and feeling within his works that the techniques of Impressionism just didn't touch, and if he didn't like a work while he was painting away from home, he would simply leave the unfinished painting behind. His early works were often referred to as "violent," due to the hasty brushstrokes involved in their composition. He spent many hours, locked away in his study, painting from memory. After meeting Pissarro, he relented to working outside on occasion and found inspiration in nature. His style and technique began to form a more structured approach, but he still favored heavy and thick brushwork. However, despite developments and a changing style and technique, he often left his paintings unfinished – he struggled greatly with whether a work was finished or not – and took months to complete projects to his own satisfaction. He was a highly analytical artist who believed that shapes could be placed together to form an overall subject. The fact that it would take him so long to work on a piece caused problems, both in terms of being able to work *en plein air* or to use real flowers and fruit, which would often wither and wilt long before he was ready for them to do so. All these difficulties may point to why he used various subjects time and time again. Around 1900, just six years before his death, Cézanne began to garner recognition for the "modernist" that he was. He was a revolutionary who "ripped up the rule book," and made up his own rules, to suit the style and nature of what he believed to be geometric realism.

Cézanne garnered a great following in his later years, and due to his modern approach – essentially before its time – he influenced a number of younger artists with his geometric style of painting. He was reluctant to meet these avid devotees, however, and was often hostile to uninvited guests (and, at times, even invited ones). Emile Bernard, an artist who was friends with both Gauguin and Van Gogh, was inspired by the geometric style and by Cézanne's ability to break down geometric forms, while Maurice Denis, working in the early 1900s, was part of the

11

■ **ABOVE: A portrait of painter Emile Bernard, by Toulouse-Lautrec. Bernard was inspired by Cézanne's work.**

"Nabi" movement – he was one of the first artists to paint in a flat style and chose, like Cézanne, to interpret nature in his own way rather than copying it. Charles Camoin, it is cited, was in awe of Cézanne, while Matisse and Pablo Picasso are known to have taken influences from him. His use of still life as subject matter revolutionized the industry, and *Apples and Oranges*, with its tendency toward the abstract and its distortion of the plane, is said to have influenced both Picasso and Georges Braque to invent the Cubism movement.

In addition to an exhibition held in 1907, Cézanne's recognition and fame were assured by Roger Fry, who held the seminal exhibition of Post-Impressionist works at the Grafton Galleries in London. It was Fry who coined the phrase Post-Impressionism, in order to give Cézanne's works some distinction from those of the Impressionists. The commercial success of the exhibition, combined with Fry's observations and writings, surely cemented Cézanne's place and legacy as the "Father of Modernism."

■ **RIGHT:** Art critic Roger Fry.

■ **BELOW:** Self-portrait (1916) of the painter Maurice Denis, in the Vasari Corridor. His family are in the background.

(PA Photos)

(Finsiel/Alinari Archives – Reproduced with the permission of Ministero per i Beni e le Attivit… Cult)

Cézanne

A Biography

(Mary Evans/Epic/Tallandier)

■ **ABOVE:** Portrait of the French painter Paul Cézanne in 1904 in Aix en Provence.

The name Cézanne may well have been Italian in origin, but Paul Cézanne was born to French parents in Aix-en-Provence, in Provence in the South of France, on January 19, 1839. His parents, Louis-Auguste Cézanne (1798-1886) and Anne Aubert (1814-1897), had their newborn son baptized just over a month after his birth, in the local parish church. Cézanne's father was a former milliner, turned banker, who co-founded a prosperous firm that afforded his son a lifetime of financial security – a situation often not available to artists in the 19th and 20th centuries, although he did have several years of financial hardship. While Cézanne's father would at first reject his son's ambitions, his mother, whom he resembled, gave him encouragement and support. She was a vivacious woman who sent Paul and his two younger sisters to school in the family's hometown of Cesana (now West Piedmont).

(PA Photos)

■ **ABOVE:** A portrait by Cézanne of his father, painted in 1866.

When he was 10 years old, Cézanne attended a school in Aix before moving to College Bourbon three years later. It was here that he met Émile Zola, an aspiring writer who would become his long-time friend. Cézanne stayed for six years, before attending the Free Municipal School of Drawing in Aix. He studied under Joseph Gilbert, a Spanish monk but, in 1858, began his law studies at the University of Aix, which was what his father expected of him. During his two years at university Cézanne realized that his dream was to be an artist; he had been taking drawing lessons alongside his law studies. His father was particularly disappointed and angry when Cézanne announced that he was leaving for Paris in 1861, however, Zola's influence had prevailed and the young artist left Aix for a new life and what he hoped would be a blossoming career. He moved to Paris to join Zola, with whom he spent a great deal of time, and eventually his father relented and was reconciled with the young rebel.

■ **ABOVE:** A cartoon of the French novelist Émile Zola, by Théobald Chartran in *Vanity Fair* magazine, 1880.

(Mary Evans/Epic/PVDE)

■ **ABOVE: Camille Pissarro and Paul Cézanne,
probably in Pontoise at Pissarro's, c. 1875.**

After joining the Académie Suisse, Cézanne met Camille Pissarro, an exciting new artist who would become his friend and mentor. Pissarro was an Impressionist painter and encouraged Cézanne to venture out of his dark surroundings and experience the life and nature that was on offer to young talented artists. It was Pissarro's influence on Cézanne that was to make a huge difference to his work. While Cézanne still preferred working indoors and using the darker tones, which he "violently" executed on canvas, he was open to trying new techniques and experimenting with colors. To begin with, Cézanne worked as student under Pissarro's tutelage, but over the next 10 years this changed to more of an equal partnership on joint painting excursions. Cézanne's first exhibition came at the Salon des Refusés in 1863, while the Paris Salon refused his works each and every year between 1864 and 1869. His paintings were considered too controversial, and were ridiculed by critics and mocked by the public as they

■ **ABOVE:** **Camille Pissarro and his wife Julie Vellay in 1877.**

■ **ABOVE:** **Cézanne had his work repeatedly refused by the Paris Salon.**

■ **ABOVE:** Vincent Van Gogh influenced Cézanne's style and technique.

20

(PA Photos)

■ **ABOVE:** Jas de Bouffan, where Cézanne lived for 40 years in Aix-en-Provence in the South of France.

did not conform to the accepted contemporary art of the time.

However, returning to Cézanne's early time in Paris, after his first five months in the city, he returned home at his father's request, having failed to gain any critical success. While back at home in Aix he joined his father's firm as a banker, but this also didn't work out for the aspiring artist. He continued to have drawing lessons at the local art school and decided to move back to Paris in 1862. Having failed the entrance exam to the Ecole des Beaux-Arts, he worked on his own projects between Paris and home, and it was at this time that he began submitting works to the Salon. Cézanne began living with Hortense Fiquet in 1869. He managed to avoid military service in the Franco-Prussian war by retreating with his mistress to L'Estaque until 1871. The following year, the couple moved

to Auvers-sur-Oise to live with Pissarro following the birth of their son, Paul, at the home of Dr. Gachet, a great admirer of Cézanne's works. Pissarro proved to be one of Cézanne's biggest influences, but Van Gogh, whom he met some time in 1873, also influenced him. It was after meeting Van Gogh that Cézanne's brushstrokes became less dense and more fluid. He was certainly using more Impressionist techniques at this time, but his interest and need to work indoors continued and he felt compelled to paint a number of still life subjects, including flowers.

With Pissarro's encouragement, Cézanne entered a number of paintings to the first and third Impressionist exhibitions in Paris in 1874 and 1877; however, he decided not to submit any works for the fourth exhibition in 1879 due to differences with his peers. He did, though, have a painting accepted by the Paris Salon in 1882. It would prove to be the first and last time this would happen. His style by this time had changed and he was moving away from the Impressionists and the Impressionist techniques. He had, since the late 1870s, begun to introduce an analysis of the scene before him, rather than creating a copy as the Impressionists did.

Cézanne was a struggling artist up until 1886, when the death of his father saw him inherit a rather large fortune, around 400,000 Francs ($500,000), as well as part of the estate of Jas de Bouffan, the Cézanne family home. Up to this point, Cézanne had only received a meager allowance from his father (around 200 francs a month), due to his relationship with his mistress Hortense Fiquet, and the fact that the couple had had a child outside of marriage. For all the years that Cézanne and Hortense were in a relationship they had managed to hide it from Cézanne Senior, however, he found out in 1878 by chance and immediately cut his son's allowance in half. Cézanne and Hortense eventually married in April 1886, just six months before his father's death in the October that year, leading to a short reconciliation. During the difficult times before reconciliation, Cézanne had written to his childhood friend Zola on a number of occasions asking for financial help in the form of loans, both for himself and other artists living in poverty. However, some income for Cézanne came in the form of other friends and patrons. Customs official and art collector, Victor Chocquet, bought a large number of Cézanne's paintings, and he also became friends with renowned art critic Gustave Geffroy and artist Auguste Rodin. Zola, meanwhile, was gaining increased recognition and had successfully established himself as a writer on the Paris scene. But, Cézanne and Zola were to fall out and their relationship would come to an end.

In 1886, Cézanne was deeply hurt by the publication of Zola's novel, *L'Oeuvre,* in which the protagonist, Claude Lantier, struggles to paint a great work. It was a fictional account of the relationship between Cézanne and Zola, which the artist chose to see as hugely personal. Like Cézanne, the protagonist is a revolutionary artist whose work is misunderstood by a scathing public only interested in traditional art. This story of an artist, unable to break into the art world to critical acclaim, was deeply hurtful to Cézanne and the book was blamed for the breakup of his friendship with the novelist. After thanking his former friend for sending him a copy, no further correspondence exists between the two men.

Following the exhibitions of 1874 and 1877, only a few of Cézanne's paintings were shown at a few well-selected venues. It wasn't until 1895, when Ambroise Vollard arranged the artist's first solo exhibition, that Cézanne began to come to the fore. The Parisian art dealer helped to ensure that Cézanne began to gain not just in recognition but financial status too, however, he was somewhat isolated – by choice – and often preferred to paint from his home in the South of France. Vollard, having been persuaded by Pissarro to arrange the solo exhibition, was to be the most important figure in Cézanne's impact on the Paris art scene. Around 150 works were included in the exhibition, resulting in increased sales (Vollard was reported to have bought every one of them) and dialogue about this groundbreaking artist

■ ABOVE: A painting of Hortense Fiquet called *Madame Cézanne*, c. 1883-1885, oil on canvas. Kunsthaus, Zurich.

from the south. When Chocquet died in 1899, many of his possessions were auctioned and art dealer, Paul Durand-Ruel, acquired the paintings that he had bought from Cézanne. In 1900, Durand-Ruel sent 12 of Cézanne's works to Berlin for an exhibition arranged by Paul Cassirer. It was the first exhibition on Cézanne held in Germany, although at that time there were no resulting sales. Cézanne found more acceptance in Belgium, while he stayed in Aix and concentrated on his main genres of still life, portraits, studies of bathers, and landscapes. Here, too, he struggled to become accepted by a public unaccustomed to "modern" art. In fact, despite the continued misunderstood nature of Cézanne's works in certain quarters, he was beginning to gain favor in numerous corners of Europe. He made his only journey outside of France in 1890 when he visited Switzerland.

Cézanne continued to paint from the family home, Jas de Bouffan, between 1895, when he moved there permanently, and 1897, when the death of his mother forced the sale of the estate so that the inheritance could be shared with his two younger sisters. He had ventured into the countryside in October 1906 and was working in a field when he was caught in a storm. He worked for another two hours before deciding to make his way home. He collapsed before he got there and was taken home by a passerby. He regained consciousness but had contracted pneumonia. Cézanne returned to work the following day but collapsed again and was returned to bed. This time he stayed there and died a few days later on October 23. He was buried just a short distance from where he was born.

Cézanne received critical acclaim and his works began to flourish. A posthumous exhibition including 56 works was held in 1907 at the Salon d'Automne and proved extremely popular. Henry Moore was cited as saying that when he saw *The Large Bathers* in 1922, it was one of the most significant moments of his life. Cézanne is widely regarded as the precursor of modern painting and is seen to have had a great deal of influence in Cubism and the Fauvism movements and, today, his work can sell for millions of dollars.

(Mary Evans/Epic/Tallandier)

■ **LEFT: Cézanne painting in Aix, 1906.**

Great Works

Paintings

A Modern Olympia

(1873)

• Oil on canvas, 18.1 in x 21.7 in (46 cm x 55 cm)

Cézanne, Paul (1839-1906): A Modern Olympia. Paris, Musée d'Orsay. © 2013. Photo Scala, Florence

When Edouard Manet unveiled his controversial *Olympia* (1863) at the 1865 Salon, it was considered a scandal. The artist reworked Titian's *Venus of Urbino*, 1538, in order to create his own vision of the work and replaced red curtains for green and green bed for red, while the faithful dog in the original was replaced by a Baudelairean cat, a symbol of promiscuity. Cézanne "modernized" Manet's work and included his own contrasts. The 1863 work included a wrapped bouquet of exquisite flowers and a delicate, arching cat, which Cézanne identifies by an explosion of blooms in a huge ornamental vase and a small scruffy dog with a red collar. In his portrayal, the staid prostitute and her maid are also treated with more enthusiasm. Instead of reclining rather majestically, the prostitute is curled and awkwardly naked, while the black maid – originally cradling the bouquet – is now seen "unveiling" the woman on the bed and given a much more "active" task. The work shows more expressive characters, yet they are much more ungainly than Manet's figures in Cézanne's continuing, but early, acquaintance with Impressionism. In this *Modern Olympia*, the audience is cordially invited to be spectators, while in Manet's work, the audience is only hinted at by the partially open door in the background. Cézanne had reworked Manet's piece earlier in 1870, at a time when he was highly influenced by the old masters and the paintings of Delacroix, Daumier, and Courbet. This second version was different in its use of color and more flamboyant style. He produced *A Modern Olympia* (1873) following a heated discussion with Dr. Gachet at Auvers-sur-Oise, which may have contributed to this more daring interpretation. The man in this portrayal could, it might be argued, be the artist himself, who greatly adds to the theatrical nature of the work. The painting was shown at the first Impressionist exhibition of 1874 where it was met with scorn from critics and the public alike. At the time, the work was much misunderstood.

Achille Emperaire

(1868-1870)

Cézanne, Paul (1839-1906): Achille Emperaire. Paris, Musee d'Orsay. © 2013. Photo Scala, Florence

Achille Emperaire, an artist, hailed from the same birthplace as Cézanne and was his senior by 10 years. They first met at the studio of Charles Suisse in Paris in the early 1860s and became close friends. *Achille Emperaire* is an early portrait that has been compared to Ingres' portrait of the *Emperor Napoleon I on his Imperial Throne* (1806), an oil on canvas that was much reproduced in the mid-19th century. It is known that Cézanne was particularly drawn by Napoleon, so the fact that he would choose to base a work of his own on the Emperor while incorporating someone of whom he was fond, is perhaps unsurprising. Here, like Napoleon, Emperaire (the name could have also had an influence), is sat in an over-large chair. It is the same patterned armchair that Cézanne used in an earlier portrait of his father. The chair appears to dwarf the painter from Aix and his feet are rested on a footstool, as they do not reach the ground. Ingres' portrait of Napoleon shows a much more dominant figure. In this painting, Emperaire looks rather diminished and uncomfortable, almost forlorn. The chair is very much the dominant interest in the piece, which portrays a rather sickly and deformed man.

In the painting, on the contrary, Cézanne emphasizes Emperaire's sickliness and deformed body with its fragile legs. The 1870 Salon refused the life-size painting.

Apples and Oranges
(c. 1900)

• Oil on canvas, 29.1 in x 36.6 in (74 cm x 93 cm)

Cézanne, Paul (1839-1906): Still Life with Apples and Oranges. Paris, Musee d'Orsay. © 2013. Photo Scala, Florence

Apples and Oranges belongs to the later years, where still life compositions began to occupy an essential place in Cézanne's work, and forms part of a series of six. The works were created in the artist's studio in Paris in 1899 where they feature themes of floral jug and earthenware dishes. The use of the draped cloth – reminiscent of Flemish 17th-century works – helps to define the dishes and fruit. It is essentially a pictorial approach and widely regarded as one of the most important still life pieces that Cézanne produced. For all its simplicity in its subject, the painting is an exquisite portrayal.

Bather and Rocks

(1868)

Cézanne, Paul (1839-1906): Baigneur et rocher, 1868. Norfolk (VA), Chrysler Museum. © 2013. White Images/Scala, Florence

This abstract painting of a heavy-set nude male, showing the figure with his back to the audience, holds a great deal of turbulence. The heavy black contours show just a portion of a larger painting, *Landscape with Bather*, which was produced directly onto plaster walls in the salon of the Jas de Bouffan mansion, located on the outskirts of Aix-en-Provence, in oils. It was commonplace for four years, from 1860, for Cézanne to paint directly onto the walls of the family home. Several of the works painted at this time remained there until the artist's death. It was one year later, in 1907, that Louis Granel, the then owner of Jas de Bouffan, suggested taking the paintings off the walls. This was so that they could be presented to the government for purchase. Art collector Jos Hessel purchased some of the 12 works in 1912. Of the 12 works 22 canvases were produced, of which this is one.

Boy in a Red Vest

(1889)

• Oil on canvas, 31.5 in x 25.4 in (80 cm x 64.5 cm)

Cézanne, Paul (1839-1906): The Boy in the Red Waistcoat. Zurich, Buehrle Found. © 2013. Photo Scala, Florence

Cézanne was not in the habit of signing or dating his work, however, this boy, known to be Michelangelo de Rosa, was an Italian professional model that the artist used on several occasions and the work can be dated to around 1889. This is, in part, possible because the boy is painted in situ in the interior of Cézanne's studio in Paris. Dressed in a red waistcoat, he is wearing the local costume of a peasant from the Roman Campagna. At the time, Cézanne was basing himself, on and off, in Paris. The studio was at 15 quai d'Anjou – one of his temporary homes – where the artist created the "peasant" boy sitting with his head resting on one hand. The pose had been used before in *The Temptation of Saint Anthony*. As was typical of his work, the painting shows distortion by the overlong right arm. The painting obviously states that the artist had moved away from Impressionism – it is much more structured – and had turned his attentions to big, colorful planes. The piece is constructed using a number of diagonals; note the pose, legs, table, curtain, waistcoat, and wall.

On February 10, 2008, this painting, along with three others, was stolen from the E. G. Bührle Collection, Lake Zurich, Switzerland, by a gang wearing masks, shortly before the exhibition was closed to visitors for the day. One gang member ordered staff and visitors to lie on the floor at gunpoint, while his two accomplices took the four Impressionist and Post-Impressionist paintings from a wall in the Music Room. At the time of the thefts, it was considered that the paintings were not stolen to order purely because there were other more valuable paintings within the collection, although a reward of $91,000 was offered for their safe return. All four paintings were eventually recovered. This particular piece was the last to be found – hidden in the roof of a van in a joint raid by Swiss and Serbian police – in April 2012 in Belgrade. It is rumored that a buyer had been found for the painting by the gang, willing to pay around $4.6 million (although the work has a value estimated to be around $10 million). The police raid took two years to come to fruition when they intercepted the robbers before they met with the buyer.

Gardanne

(1885-1886)

• Oil on canvas, 31.5 in x 25.2 in (80 cm x 64.1 cm)

Cézanne, Paul (1839-1906): Gardanne, 1885-86. New York, Metropolitan Museum of Art. Oil on canvas, 31 1/2 x 25 1/4 in (80 x 64.1 cm). Gift of Dr. and Mrs. Franz H. Hirschland, 1957. Acc.n.: 57.181 © 2013. Image copyright The Metropolitan Museum of Art/Art Resource/Scala, Florence

At the time this painting was produced, Cézanne was spending little time in Paris. He had been deeply hurt by Zola's novel, *L'Oeuvre*, published in March 1886, and was suffering from continual rejections from the Salon. In fact, he was so depressed by the Salon's attitude to his work that he stopped submitting pieces for several years. Prior to inheriting the family home – Jas de Bouffan – he rented a house in Gardanne, a village near Aix. This painting is from that time – one of several – which showed his use of experimentation in block work. *The Village of Gardanne* (1885-1887), shows much more foliage than the picture depicted here, but it contains the same warm terracotta and mellow overtones. The painting shows a tumbling landscape, solid in its construction, yet freely flowing from the top of the canvas to the bottom. It depicts the pyramidal shapes of the buildings and complex structure and is regarded as a key transition for the artist.

It is one of three views of Gardanne, where the town is portrayed through an anticipated Cubism. Cézanne found serenity in Gardanne, where he formed friendships and little Paul attended the local school for boys. However, the move here brought about the end of his long-time friendship with Émile Zola.

Landscape at Auvers

(1873)

• Oil on canvas, 18.2 in x 21.7 in (46.3 cm x 55.2 cm)

Cézanne, Paul (1839-1906): Le Quartier du Four, Auvers-sur-Oise (Landscape, Auvers), c. 1873. Philadelphia, Philadelphia Museum of Art. Oil on canvas, 18 1/4 x 21 3/4 in (46.3 x 55.2 cm). The Samuel S. White 3rd and Vera White Collection, 1967. © 2013. Photo The Philadelphia Museum of Art/Art Resource/Scala, Florence

Cézanne's broad, panoramic views of the countryside were immortalized and framed with branches and foliage – as seen here – as well as architecture. His paintings of the Provençal countryside rarely saw human activity and it's hard to imagine that these still life works were not produced while the artist surveyed the view. In fact, these landscapes were manipulated from the original in order to fit the canvas in the way Cézanne wanted them. He understood that the changing light along the contours of the subject would never allow him to do the work full justice, and so he chose to transfer the images as best he could with his own interpretation.

It is this way of working that set him apart from other Impressionists. He continued with his beliefs in interpreting nature through art during his later years, where he used color in equal intensity throughout his compositions. He often worked and reworked his paintings, and it is cited that the reason he rarely signed his works was that he considered them unfinished. During the last 10 years of his life Cézanne's paintings were more simplified, with components consisting of spheres, cones, and cylinders. It was these works that brought about his reputation with regard to an anticipated Cubism – he changed the complex and imperfect forms of nature into defined and essential shapes. Today, the brilliance of what Cézanne achieved is highly revered, but more than 100 years ago he was an artist ahead of his time.

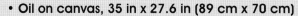

• Oil on canvas, 35 in x 27.6 in (89 cm x 70 cm)

Madame Cézanne in a red dress (Madame Cézanne en robe rouge), 1890, by Paul Cézanne (1839-1906), oil on canvas, 89 x 70 cm. Sao Paulo, Museu de Arte de Sao Paulo.
© 2013. DeAgostini Picture Library/Scala, Florence

This portrait of Hortense Fiquet, Cezanne's mistress who became his wife, is a little rigid in its portrayal, although it is a beautiful painting. The artist has not romanticized her, however, and her face is shown as plain. The portrait appears more as a composition rather than as a romantic idealism of the woman herself. It is almost as if the subject of the painting – the red dress – is an excuse for the artist to experiment with the color, and the sitter is almost surplus to requirements save for the fact that her inclusion is necessary as the wearer of the clothing. The painting portrays a carefully arranged still life, rather than a person who meant a great deal to the artist. The composition is rather asymmetrical, apart from the face tilting to the right and therefore only allowing one ear to show.

Mont Sainte-Victoire looking towards Lauves

(1902-1906)

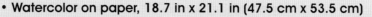

• Watercolor on paper, 18.7 in x 21.1 in (47.5 cm x 53.5 cm)

Cézanne, Paul (1839-1906). Mount Sainte-Victoire looking towards Lauves; La Montagne Sainte Victoire Vue des Lauves. c. 1902-1906. London, Private Coll. watercolor on paper. 47.5 x 53.5cm. © 2013. Christies' Images, London/Scala, Florence

Cézanne painted 28 watercolors of Mont Sainte-Victoire between 1900 and 1906. Most of them were painted from the studio he built in Les Lauves, in 1902, just north of Aix, looking across the valley. From here, he had a magnificent view of the imposing mountain – a spectacular backdrop – against the swirling foliage in the foreground. Cézanne had experimented with watercolors throughout his career, but the majority was produced in the final decade of his life. His method was remarkable, and completely different from that of his peers. His method was, in fact, fairly complicated in that he began on the shadow with a single patch, which was overlapped with a second, and a third, etc., until all the tints were hinged to one another. It was this method that helped Cézanne create not just the form of the subject but the color of it too. In many of these watercolors there was the merest hint of a pencil outline, over which the artist laid these overlapping patches of color. Each layer was allowed to dry before another was applied. Also in these landscapes, the artist allows the unpainted areas to "shine" by appearing in their whiteness to provide the brilliance of sunlight.

Mont Sainte-Victoire

(1902-1904)

• Oil on canvas, 28.7 in x 36.2 in (73 cm x 91.9 cm)

Cézanne, Paul (1839-1906): Mont Sainte-Victoire, 1902-04. Philadelphia, Philadelphia Museum of Art. Oil on canvas, 28 3/4 x 36 3/16 in (73 x 91.9 cm). The George W. Elkins Collection, 1936. © 2013. Photo The Philadelphia Museum of Art/Art Resource/Scala, Florence

This stunning landscape of Mont Sainte-Victoire symbolizes, in one of the 60 works he created of the subject, a favorite motif. This painting pays homage to the earth, mountain, and sky. The houses, roads, and trees are indicated only by patches of color, while the foreground is almost completely obliterated. The uninterrupted view that Cézanne had of the mountain from his studio was described in a letter, in 1904, to Bernard where "Lines parallel to the horizon give breadth..." By this time, Cézanne had fully embraced Catholicism, and it is entirely possible that he truly believed that the harmony and serenity he found in his landscapes was God-given. Perhaps in a nod to religious beliefs, the mountain points to heaven, although there are no obvious religious elements in the painting.

Pastoral
(1870)

• **Oil on canvas, 25.6 in x 31.9 in (65 cm x 81 cm)**

Cézanne, Paul (1839-1906): Pastoral. Paris, Musee d'Orsay. © 2013. Photo Scala, Florence

This painting had a number of different titles before becoming simply *Pastoral*. It was originally entitled *Picnic at the Seaside* before becoming known as *Plein-Air Scene, Don Quixote on the Barbary Shore,* and *Idyll* by those seeking to analyze the piece. The painting is Cézanne's representation of Manet's *Le Dejeuner sur L'herbe*. It was another of Manet's works to cause scandal at the Salon, as had *Olympia*, and Cézanne was just as careful here to interpret his own contrasts as he did with *The Modern Olympia*. Here (just as in the Olympian paintings) the women of the piece are naked, while the men are clothed. However, Cézanne incorporates a deep lake, a steep shoreline, and large trees. His rendition is perhaps more adventurous and, again, he paints himself. This time, however, he is not merely seated as a spectator, but reclining in a relaxed pose in the center of the piece and not off to the side. The figure is completely indifferent to the nude bathers. It has been suggested that Baudelaire (the French poet) and Wagner (the German composer), who were much discussed at the time of this work, were also important in its composition, although it is clear that Manet is the overriding influence. The piece is Phantasm, where the women pose like nymphs, Antiope and Venus. There is a still quality to this piece that suggests that any turmoil there might be has been completely banished.

Pierrot and Harlequin (Mardi Gras)
(1888)

Cézanne, Paul (1839-1906): Shrove Tuesday. Moscow, Pushkin Museum. © 2013. Photo Scala, Florence

Pierrot and Harlequin (Mardi Gras) is perhaps not as well known as *Harlequin*, however, this is one of Cézanne's most important works with figures. It portrays the artist's 17-year-old son as the confident Harlequin. The theme first influenced the artist in the form of a 17th-century painting in the museum at Aix.

Cézanne painted four works with Commedia dell'Arte (Comedy of Craft) themes, including three single Harlequins and the picture depicted here. This particular painting is probably the most descriptive of the four works and was possibly the first, although there is no concrete evidence of this. The painting shows the two figures against the backdrop of the curtain, suggesting the presence of the stage, somewhere out of sight. In the 19th century, carnivals were popular in Paris, and the artist first painted his son in a Harlequin costume in 1888. However, carnivals, having been banished for 100 years, were reintroduced to Aix in late 1890 and may have re-influenced the artist around this time.

Cézanne's Harlequin works were known to have influenced Picasso; one painting that attests to this is his *Harlequin with Half Mask*, 1918.

Portrait of Dominique Aubert, the Artist's Uncle

(1866)

• Oil on canvas, 31.4 in x 25.2 in (79.7 cm x 64.1 cm)

Cézanne, Paul (1839-1906): Dominique Aubert, the Artist's Uncle, 1866. New York, Metropolitan Museum of Art. Oil on canvas, 31 3/8 x 25 1/4 in (79.7 x 64.1 cm). Wolfe Fund, 1951; acquired from The Museum of Modern Art, Lillie P. Bliss Collection. Acc.n.: 53.140.1. © 2013. Image copyright The Metropolitan Museum of Art/Art Resource/Scala, Florence

It would be hard not to see the family resemblance in this portraiture of Cézanne's maternal uncle, Dominique Aubert. The artist's uncle was happy to sit for his nephew and there are at least nine portraits of Aubert. He was even prepared to wear costumes in order to further Cézanne's work. The artist was feared by a large number of his sitters because he made them stay absolutely still – this helped to give his portraitures the quality of still life pieces, but his demands were fairly harsh for his subjects. Many have suggested that the reason that Cézanne's portraiture subjects look so tired and somber is because they probably sat for many, many hours – he was said to be a slow painter. Ambroise Vollard sat for 115 sessions for one painting. The painting was eventually abandoned – because the artist was dissatisfied with the result – and he told the sitter that he would eventually find the correct color.

Rocks above Château Noir

(c. 1904)

• Oil on canvas, 25.6 in x 21.3 in (65 cm x 54 cm)

Cézanne, Paul (1839-1906): Rocher pres des grottes au dessus du chateau noir, 1904. Paris, Musee d'Orsay. Dim. 0.65 X 0.54 m. © 2013. White Images/Scala, Florence

At the turn of the 20th century, when Cézanne returned to his hometown, it was here that he found tranquility in Mont Sainte-Victoire and the Bibémus quarries. These subjects were to appear in many of his works and become part of his experimentation up to the time of his death. In this painting, the artist depicts a pile of rocks and tree trunks. The rocks and the trees frame the painting and help to bring the subject up close and personal with the audience. In this painting, the brush strokes are fairly allusive and helped to add to an increasingly subtle, timeless vision achieved by Cézanne. The use of colors in his unique approach was to become an essential foundation for modern paintings of the 20th century. The painting was acquired by Matisse, who noted that Cézanne's use of colors provided: "a force within a painting."

This work, produced two years before his death, is a solid representation and celebration of the countryside around his home. It reflects a time when he was obsessed with color – in order to give form and presence – and solidity. It shows how he wanted to portray the forces of the earth and, despite the "stillness" of the piece, there is much movement and the suggestion that it is only a matter of time before the rocks move ever downward. Again, without the obvious religious reference, there is still a nod to the relationship that the artist had found with God at this time. For Cézanne, these landscapes represented artistic inspiration coupled with a spiritual serenity.

Still Life with a Watermelon and Pomegranates

(1900-1906)

- **Watercolor over graphite on laid paper, 12.4 in x 19.2 in (31.4 cm x 48.8 cm)**

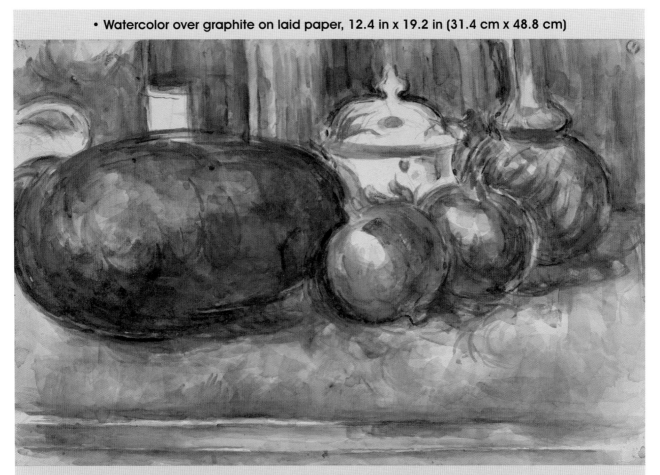

Cézanne, Paul (1839-1906): Still-Life with a Watermelon and Pomegranates, 1900-1906. New York, Metropolitan Museum of Art. Watercolor over graphite on laid paper, sheet: 12 3/8 x 19 3/16 in (31.4 x 48.8 cm). The Walter H. and Leonore Annenberg Collection, Gift of Walter H. and Leonore Annenberg, 2001, Bequest of Walter H. Annenberg, 2002. Inv. 2001.202.1. © 2013. Image copyright The Metropolitan Museum of Art/Art Resource/Scala, Florence

This work consists of five rounded objects, including a melon, two pomegranates, a carafe, and a white sugar bowl – which also appears in *Dish of Apples*. It is an exquisite watercolor that centers its subjects on top of a table. The piece was composed using graphite to give Cézanne's theme its form before he used transparent color to literally bring this still life to prominence. The layering, shadows, and mirroring in this work are breathtaking in their composition.

He induces space, suggestion, and light by leaving elements of the canvas white; for example, note the table edge in the foreground which is completely overridden to the right of the canvas by the purple wash. There is spatial definition here while the colors give a vibrant intensity.

Still Life with Plaster Cupid

(1895)

• **Oil on paper on board, 27.6 in x 22.4 in (70 cm x 57 cm)**

Plaster Cupid and the Anatomy, 1895, by Paul Cézanne (1839-1906). London, Courtauld Institute Galleries. © 2013. DeAgostini Picture Library/Scala, Florence

This work was completed in 1895 and went on to become one of Cézanne's more famous still life paintings. It was seen as radical for the time because of its abstractive approach and points to the Cubist movement yet to come. There is clear distortion here in a work that depicts a molded, yet armless, plaster cast of Cupid stood on a table among some fruit and blue cloth in a painting which mixes everyday objects with a mystical theme. By this time, having faced rejection of his works by the Salon, Cézanne was in the process of holding a solo exhibition in collaboration with Ambroise Vollard. This piece, along with others in the exhibition, was well received by an appreciative audience who found favor in his works.

The Cupid, it appears, is in contrast to the other objects that are placed around him and there is distortion caused, it is suggested, by the fact that the artist did not paint the composition from one position. He rotated as he worked around the plaster cast and fruit in order to capture the subject from a number of angles. Having moved away from his darker shades and his personal inner turmoil, Cézanne found strength in color, however, he often utilized dark colors for shading, which he does here to great effect. It was more usual to paint apples alongside mystical figures, but here, the artist has chosen onions. Cézanne was renowned for using solid brush strokes and for painting only what he saw. This goes some way to explaining why he felt that many of his works were unfinished – he could always see something new and that last brush stroke was almost an enigma.

Sugar Bowl, Pears and Blue Cup

(1866)

- Oil on canvas, 11.8 in x 16.1 in (30 cm x 41 cm)

Cézanne, Paul (1839-1906): Sucrier, tasse bleue et poires, 1866. Aix-en-Provence, Musee Granet. Peinture. © 2013. White Images/Scala, Florence

This work signals Cézanne's interest in still life paintings from his early days. This piece uses thick swathes of paint applied with a palette knife, and shows clearly the influence of Monticelli – who also inspired Van Gogh – with its strong, blended colors. He reproduces this still life in his painting, *The Artist's Father, reading L'Evénement*, behind his seated father on the wall.

Temptations of Saint Anthony

(1875)

• Oil on canvas, 18.5 in x 22 in (47 cm x 56 cm)

Cézanne, Paul (1839-1906): La tentation de saint Antoine L'ermite saint Antoine le Grand (251-356) subit les tentations du Diable dans le desert. 1875.
Paris, Musee d'Orsay. peinture, cm 47 x 56. © 2013. White Images/Scala, Florence

Like many other artists, Cézanne depicts the temptations of Saint Anthony, inspired by Gustave Flaubert's novel. Flaubert spent much of his life working on his book, which culminated in three versions in 1849, 1856, and 1872. The final version was published two years later. Based on the famous temptation faced by Saint Anthony the Great in the Egyptian desert, the theme is often repeated in modern art. In this portrayal the central, naked, woman is holding up her arm and arching her back seductively while the devil looks on. In an early work of the same title, Cézanne almost relegates the title theme to the top left-hand corner of the work as he focuses on the three naked women who separate heaven from the fires of hell in the bottom right of the piece. It is well known that Cézanne struggled with the concept of nude models all his life and preferred to work from memory of the naked form.

The Bather

(c. 1885)

• Oil on canvas, 50 in x 38.1 in (127 cm x 96.8 cm)

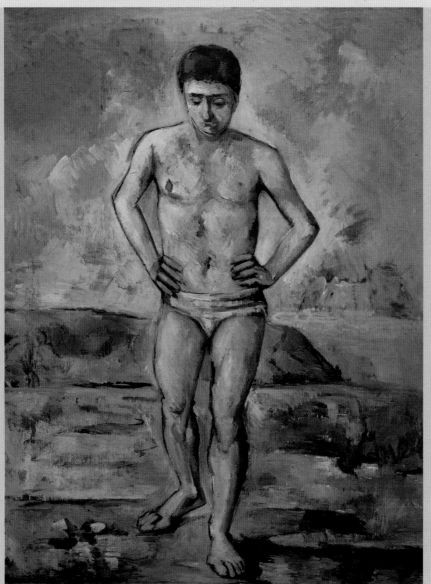

Cézanne, Paul (1839-1906): The Bather, 1885. New York, Museum of Modern Art (MoMA). Oil on canvas, 50 x 38 1/8 in (127 x 96.8 cm). Lillie P. Bliss Collection. 1.1934. © 2013. Digital image, The Museum of Modern Art, New York/Scala, Florence

This work shows a rather awkward, "squat" bather, not very muscular, and a little imprecise, yet it is highly revered as one of Cézanne's most evocative paintings of the figure. The bather's leg, to the left, is placed firmly on the ground, but he trails his right leg, and the right side of his body is higher than the left, while the right arm is somewhat distorted and elongated. The landscape behind the bather is rather barren and out of proportion, but fits in with the shadows on the body which share their colors with the air, land, and sea in hues of blue, violet, and green. The piece is solid and shows that Cézanne was moving away from traditional art and into the modern era. This monumental physical form is poised on horizontal lines. The vertical works in harmony with the horizontal. There is symmetry between the rock edge and the bent arm, and both the figure and the landscape have been given the same treatment in brushwork. This work provided inspiration for new artists at the turn of the century. Although tied to the landscape, the figure is detached and unaware.

The Blue Vase

(1883-1887)

• Oil on canvas, 24 in x 19.7 in (61 cm x 50 cm)

Cézanne, Paul (1839-1906): The Blue Vase. Paris, Musee d'Orsay. © 2013. Photo Scala, Florence

The distortion that is seen in Cézanne's landscapes and earlier works of still life is applied again in his later arrangements of objects, fruit, and flowers. The vase and the flowers are equally intense in their own rights. There is a harmony within the piece, from the green of the leaves to the vibrant colors of the flowers, which contrast yet blend beautifully with the blue vase. The off-placement of the vase allows us to see around the vase more (a fact which excited the Cubists). The vibrant blue of the vase is framed against the blue background. These and the blue touches on the table are contrasted with warmer, neutral tones. If you look carefully, the outlines of the vase may be seen – these have been carefully crafted and contrast with the fruit outlines, which lie partly aloof from the subject.

The Card Players

(1896)

• Oil on canvas, 18.9 in x 22.8 in (48 cm x 58 cm)

Cézanne, Paul (1839-1906): The Card Players. Paris, Musee d'Orsay. © 2013. Photo Scala, Florence

Cézanne found the numerous card players around his home in the South of France as timeless as he did the landscapes that surrounded the countryside in which they lived. These men, old and young alike, were to become the theme for a number of works. *Card Players* portrays a nostalgia and deep understanding for a way of life, uniquely captured in the simple act of playing cards. There is stillness to the piece, almost as if you are expected to read the thoughts of the figures so intent on their game. Here, the artist uses a balance of warm and cool colors. The principal warm is given by the red-orange table and its cover, which is surrounded by cool greens and blues. As with many works by Cézanne, there are trademark highlights on the canvas, where the unpainted canvas is allowed to show through, for example, on the hands of the participants, while proportionally there are some variants – note the knees of the left-hand player which extend beyond where perhaps they should. The table appears lopsided against the partition backdrop. It is cited that the man on the left smoking the pipe is Père Alexander, the gardener at Jas de Bouffan.

Cézanne painted five different versions of this theme. An earlier and much larger version of the *Card Players* shows five figures around the table, one of who is standing. There is no partition and the pipe in this painting is replaced by a row of four pipes on the wall. More recent interpretations have suggested that, rather than being a totally nostalgic piece, the composition might represent the struggle that Cézanne faced with his father over his painting.

The Eternal Feminine

(1877)

• Oil on canvas, 16.9 in x 20.9 in (43 cm x 53 cm)

The eternal feminine, 1877, by Paul Cézanne (1839-1906), oil on canvas, 43 x 53 cm. Malibu, J. Paul Getty Museum. © 2013. DeAgostini Picture Library/Scala, Florence

It is well known that Cézanne was uncomfortable using naked models, yet they featured so prominently in his work. He was renowned for using the drawings of nude models that he produced in Paris. This piece is no exception. In this work, the naked central woman is celebrated and adored by her devotees. How the woman actually feels about the attention is unclear: her face is virtually blank – not uncommon in Cézanne nudes. To one side an artist captures the scene on canvas. The male figures within the piece all come from different professions. Whatever the true meaning of the painting, one thing is clear: the woman is vulnerable, or a mere object to be gawped at. In 1991, the painting was returned to its original state after it was altered in 1954 in order to make the nude "less disturbing."

The Great Pine

(1890-1896)

• Oil on canvas, 35 in x 27.6 in (89 cm x 70 cm)

The large pine tree (Le gran pin), 1890-1896, by Paul Cézanne (1839-1906), oil on canvas, 89 x 70 cm. Sao Paulo, Museu de Arte de Sao Paulo.
© 2013. DeAgostini Picture Library/Scala, Florence

This exciting painting shows great movement and fluidity. The tree stands out against its smaller, less interesting or detailed peers, and reveals a dramatic scene with conflicting forms, reacting to the wind. The tree is strained, but is a simple yet carefully crafted form of nature, which reveals great art. This tree's branches are the only ones visible, while the other trees just provide support and balance to the work. The brushstrokes evoke the movement and turbulence of this powerful painting.

The Gulf of Marseilles from L'Estaque
(also called L'Estaque)

(1878-1879)

• Oil on canvas, 22.8 in x 28.3 in (58 cm x 72 cm)

Cézanne, Paul (1839-1906): L'Estaque. Paris, Musee d'Orsay. © 2013. Photo Scala, Florence

It was in his native Provence that Cézanne established his recurrent motifs and themes. He found great inspiration in the Bay at L'Estaque and it was here that he painted his first seascapes. It was a much-loved place of the artist and a sanctuary where he could escape to when he needed a rest from the stresses and strains of life in the French capital. Just as with Mont Sainte-Victoire, he used different mediums to capture his scenes here. In this work Cézanne used oil on canvas, but he also produced the scene in a number of watercolors. Once again he uses a series of short brushstrokes in order to create form and texture. He uses dark lines to outline the geometry of the manmade structures. The painting shows how the artist is moving away from Impressionism and traditional perspective. The eye is drawn to the left of the work where the bay narrows, leaving the audience to wonder what is around the corner. However, the painting is so vibrant that the audience is left wondering what is either side of the panoramic view. This "solid" painting of one of Cézanne's favorite places was of significant interest to young artists at the turn of the century, many of who visited the shores of the bay to capture it in their own images.

The House of the Hanged Man

(1873)

• Oil on canvas, 21.7 in x 26 in (55 cm x 66 cm)

Cézanne, Paul (1839-1906): La maison du pendu (The House of the Hanged Man). Auvers-sur-Oise, 1873. Paris, Musee d'Orsay. Oil on canvas, 55 x 66 cm.
© 2013. Photo Scala, Florence

This work was one of three of *The House of the Hanged Man* and exhibited at the first Impressionist exhibition in 1874. The influence of Cézanne's mentor, Camille Pissarro, can be seen in this painting, but he has kept to the paler colors favored by Impressionists, rather than the vibrant colors for which he would be universally recognized later. The subject is simple and solid, but the composition is complicated. There is a deep feeling of solitude in this painting. It could be suggested that the painting has a strong pull, urging the audience to venture downward toward the house, which is in complete contrast to the likes of Munch who was prolific in having his figures and subjects seemingly rushing toward the front of his paintings.

The Lake at Annecy

(1896)

Cézanne, Paul (1839-1906): Le lac d' Annecy. 1896. London, Courtauld Institute Galleries. peinture, 65 x 81 cm. © 2013. White Images/Scala, Florence

This impressive and exciting painting was created when Cézanne holidayed in Talloires in the summer of 1896. The view is across Lac d'Annecy toward Château de Duingt. In reality, the Château was about 1 mile away, however, here, Cézanne makes it appear closer by narrowing the visual field and by using the large tree to the left of the piece to frame it. The colors here are harmonious and work well together, almost blending tree to hillside and what might be mountain ridges with the water in the lake. Cézanne, again, uses warm and cool colors in juxtaposition in a vibrant and monumental structure. The blues and greens are accentuated by the warm hues, where the early morning sunlight reaches the trunk of the tree, the distant hills, and the architecture on the opposite shoreline. The reflections are slightly distorted, but the painting has a unified structure, carefully crafted and breathtaking in its ingenuity.

The Large Bathers
(c. 1900-1906)

• Oil on canvas, 82.9 in x 98.7 in (210.5 cm x 250.8 cm)

Cézanne, Paul (1839-1906): The Large Bathers, c. 1900-1906. Philadelphia, Philadelphia Museum of Art. © 2013. Photo The Philadelphia Museum of Art/Art Resource/Scala, Florence

This rather formal painting is the largest of Cézanne's Bathers series (of which there were three). Paolo Veronese's *The Supper at Emmaus* undoubtedly influenced Cézanne, and comparisons can be drawn between the two. Both works have figures grouped into two three-dimensional pyramids on either side of the center. In Cézanne's painting, the center section has parallel planes depicting the sand and the sea, while the figures represent heroic nudes in a natural setting. They are arranged in a variety of poses but appear – as is so natural in Cézanne's work – as still life under an arch of intersected trees, the tops of which are not visible in the painting. The figures do not portray any personality and seem structure-like in their composition. *The Large Bathers* is the artist's interpretation of the female nude. The size of this painting is huge and shows clearly that Cézanne is moving toward the abstract, although not quite there yet with this work. This was the last of the three paintings to be produced and, like the *Card Players*, represents timelessness. The intersecting trees almost represent a stage-like presence, which frames not just the nudes but also the backdrop of land and sea. The triangular effect that the trunks have draws the eye to focus on the lake and the smaller figures in the background. It is the depiction of a calm and serene world that has captured the imagination of the artist. *The Large Bathers* followed a number of practice paintings where Cézanne experimented with how the figures might relate to each other. This work is highly regarded as a masterpiece of modern art and one of the greatest compositions of all time.

The Murder
(1869-1870)

• Oil on canvas, 25.6 in x 31.9 in (65 cm x 81 cm)

Murder, 1869-1870, by Paul Cézanne (1839-1906), oil on canvas, 65 x 81 cm. Liverpool, National Museums Liverpool – Walker Art Gallery.
© 2013. DeAgostini Picture Library/Scala, Florence

This early work is a brutal portrayal of the act of murder. While the murderer holds his arm and weapon above his head, the heavy-set woman to the right of the scene pins the victim to the ground. While the murderer, with his back to the audience, and his accomplice have no faces, the victim's face is clear and contorted in pain. There is no explanation for the murder, just the focus on the act itself. It is a powerful and fairly shocking piece framed under a threatening sky and a foreboding river or sea, ready to claim the victim once the perpetrators have finished their deadly deed. It is a menacing work that belongs to a group of paintings from the 1860s in which the artist, it could be argued, is exploring his deep emotions and turbulence within his family relationships. It is a frighteningly dark painting, which allows no mercy in its harrowing take on murder. The only respite in the work is the moonlight, which brightens the arms of the murderer, accomplice, and the victim, whose right arm binds the three together in a central focus.

The Negro Scipio

(1866-1868)

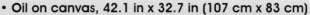

• Oil on canvas, 42.1 in x 32.7 in (107 cm x 83 cm)

The Negro Scipio, 1866-1868, by Paul Cézanne (1839-1906), oil on canvas, 107 x 83 cm. Sao Paulo, Museu de Arte de Sao Paulo. © 2013. DeAgostini Picture Library/Scala, Florence

In 1863, Cézanne joined the Académie Suisse. The circle participated at the Salon in the year that Manet exhibited *Olympia,* while Cézanne exhibited this exquisite monumental painting *The Negro Scipio.* The model, Scipio, was an extremely popular subject at the studio of Académie Suisse. Cézanne painted the muscular subject, articulated with swirling brushstrokes. He used tones of black, bronze, and blue against the contrasting white fabric triangle on which the model is leaning. The contrasts in the work are strong: the muscled man against fragile cloth, with his strong body giving in to the delicate fabric. The face, in shadow, gives an element of mystery to the piece. Monet became the initial owner of this painting and hung the work in his bedroom.

The Painter's Father, Louis-Auguste Cézanne

(c. 1865)

- **Oil on house paint on plaster mounted on canvas scrim, 66 in x 45 in (167.6 cm x 114.3 cm)**

Cézanne, Paul (1839-1906): The Painter's Father, Louis-Auguste Cézanne, c. 1865. London, National Gallery. Oil on house paint on plaster mounted on canvas scrim, 167.6 x 114.3 cm. Bought, 1968. Acc.n.: 3989. © 2013. Copyright The National Gallery, London/Scala, Florence

Like a number of other paintings, this one was painted directly onto a wall at Jas de Bouffan, bought by Cézanne's father in 1859. The artist's father is thought to have been in his early sixties when the piece was composed using a palette knife. The strokes used were quick and aggressive.

The Railway Cutting
(c. 1870)

• Oil on canvas, 31.7 in x 50.9 in (80.4 cm x 129.4 cm)

Cézanne, Paul (1839-1906): The Railway Cutting, c. 1870 (in the background the Montagne Sainte Victoire). Munich, Neue Pinakothek Muenchen, Bayerische Staatsgemaeldesammlungen. Oil on canvas, 80.4 x 129.4 cm. Inv.: 8646. © 2013. Photo Scala, Florence/BPK, Bildagentur fuer Kunst, Kultur und Geschichte, Berlin

Influenced by the steam trains that ran close to Jas de Bouffan, Cézanne worked on a number of railway subjects while he lived in Aix. This particular work was an early experiment in different types of landscape composition. *The Railway Cutting* shows the railway cutting at the center of the piece with a signal box, while both sides of the canvas balance the apparent equilibrium, with Mont Sainte-Victoire to the right in undulating landscape and a house on a small hill to the left. Although the artist would return to the mountain motif many times, this was the first time he focused on the mountain in its own right. While he concentrates on the railway line between Aix-Rognac, and went on to depict the railway in a number of landscape subjects, including viaducts and railway buildings, he chose not to include the steam trains for which these lines were built. This was unusual in terms of Impressionism, where steam trains were often the central focus.

Three Skulls on an Oriental Rug
(1898)

• Oil on canvas, 15.4 in x 18.3 in (39 cm x 46.5 cm)

Cézanne, Paul (1839-1906): Trois cranes sur un tapis oriental, 1898. Solothurn, Kunstmuseum. © 2013. White Images/Scala, Florence

Skulls are often used in still life to symbolize how short time is in human existence. Cézanne was a frequent painter of human skulls and, in this piece, uses three skulls, arranged almost like still life apples, in a pyramid on an Oriental rug. The work is quite haunting in its approach to death, and here, he builds up a complex network of color where the skulls contrast with the richness of the rug beneath them. Cézanne used a gradual accumulation of colors in order to "build" the composition. The painting is dark and forbidding; it is morbid, yet compelling.

Woman with a Coffeepot

(c .1895)

- Oil on canvas, 51.2 in x 37.8 in (130 cm x 96 cm)

Cézanne, Paul (1839-1906): La femme a la cafetiere. c. 1895. Paris, Musee d'Orsay. peinture, cm 130 x 96. © 2013. White Images/Scala, Florence

The woman depicted in this still life has never been identified, but it is thought she could have been a servant at Jas de Bouffan. Cézanne used few professional models and preferred to use people he knew, including family members. It is cited that this was because he was shy and painted rather slowly. This monumental painting is timeless and has universality. The woman sits "lost in time," next to a coffee pot and spoon in a cup, all erect and still, yet the work suggests movement: the pleats in her dress, her face turned toward the table, the fold in the table covering, and the floral screen to the left of the canvas. Having said that, this work is more a study of forms rather than of character; note the blank expression of the woman and the hands resting lightly on her lap.

The painting is simple in its composition and follows a rigid arrangement of horizontal and vertical lines: from the screen, the paneling behind the woman, the pleats, and even the shadowing on the woman's face. This geometrical approach all points toward Cubism and shows a shift in Cézanne's work.

Young Girl at the Piano – Overture to Tannhäuser, Portrait of the Artist's Sister and Mother

(1868)

• Oil on canvas, 22.4 in x 36.2 in (57 cm x 92 cm)

Cézanne, Paul (1839-1906): Girl at the Piano (Tannhaeuser Overture). St. Petersburg, Hermitage Museum. © 2013. Photo Scala, Florence

As an earlier work, this painting of the artist's mother and sister is relatively dark, however, it has life and vitality, although it does not have the brushstrokes of an Impressionist. It shows the artist's personality in both style and content. The reference to Wagner's music (the *Overture to Tannhäuser* was a Wagner composition that was later added as a subtitle to this painting) conjures up the powerful and the emotional, and helps to reinforce the artist's own temperament. There is a sobriety and detachment in the piece, painted at a time when several early portraits were also composed, made forceful by the use of a palette knife.

Self-portrait with Palette

(1885-1887)

• Oil on canvas, 36.2 in x 28.7 in (92 cm x 73 cm)

Self Portrait with Palette, 1885-1887, by Paul Cézanne (1839-1906), Private Coll. © 2013. DeAgostini Picture Library/Scala, Florence

Cézanne made more than 20 self-portraits. While other artists may have used themselves as models – for example Van Gogh – due to financial constraints, it seems more likely that Cézanne used his own image due to the slowness of his work; few sitters, apart from his wife, Hortense, were prepared to sit for the many hours required.

As was usual in the artist's self-portraits, he gives no indication of his mood through his facial expression. This self-portrait is particularly impersonal, in fact, the face and eyes are unfinished. In all his portraits Cézanne is unconcerned with character and personality, he is more focused on achieving a unified painting that uses a single type of brushstroke, with diagonal lines applied evenly across the canvas. It would prove to be a brushstroke that he would develop and apply to his work across subjects and themes.

The artist stands behind his easel and palette and the subject is composed and framed using a series of rectangles. This includes the head and body, framed perfectly within the easel and palette, while the colors are balanced. The head's tones are closely related to these objects too, as is the jacket. The face is somewhat rectangular, while the hair and beard mirror the rounded corner of the palette. The theme of connections is continued through the vertical edge of the palette and the sleeve, parallel to the frame. The table, in the bottom left of the painting, is a moment of Cubism within the piece. The overall affect is one of isolation, rigid in its approach, yet Cézanne has made a bold composition of himself. However, the rectangular nature of the work keeps the audience at arm's length; it keeps them back. There is nothing on the flat surface to draw the audience in.

Cézanne

In The 21st Century

For further information and where to visit, the following organizations, institutions, museums, and galleries house the works of Cézanne in the 21st century.

USA

Barnes Foundation, Merion, PA
www.barnesfoundation.org
Sixty paintings including Leda and The Swan

Metropolitan Museum of Art, New York
www.metmuseum.org
Twenty-three paintings including Bathers

National Gallery of Art, Washington, DC
www.nga.gov
Twenty-two paintings

Philadelphia Museum of Art, Philadelphia, PA
www.philamuseum.org
Fourteen paintings

Museum of Modern Art, New York
www.moma.org
Eleven paintings

The Art Institute, Chicago
www.artic.edu/aic/index.php
Nine paintings

Solomon R. Guggenheim Museum, New York
www.guggenheim.org/new_york
Seven paintings

The Philips Collection, Washington, DC
www.philipscollection.org
Six paintings

Fogg Art Museum, Harvard University, Cambridge, MA
www.artmuseums.harvard.edu/fogg/
Five paintings

Museum of Fine Arts, Boston, MA
www.mfa.org
Five paintings

Detroit Institute of Arts, Detroit, MI
www.dia.org
Five paintings

Museum of Art, Rhode Island School of Design, Providence, RI
www.risd.edu/museum.cfm
Four paintings

Yale University Art Gallery, New Haven, CT
www.artgallery.yale.edu
Four paintings

The Norton Simon Museum, Norton, Pasadena, California
www.nortonsimon.org
Four paintings

Cleveland Museum of Art, Cleveland, Ohio
www.clevelandart.org
Three paintings

Los Angeles County Museum of Art, LA
www.lacma.org
Three paintings

J. Paul Getty Museum, Malibu, California
www.getty.edu/museum
Three paintings

Carnegie Museum of Art, Carnegie Institute, Pittsburgh, PA
www.cmoa.org
Three paintings

Saint Louis Art Museum, Saint Louis, MO
www.stlouis.art.museum
Three paintings

Baltimore Museum of Art, Baltimore, MD
www.artbma.org
Two paintings

Museum of Fine Arts, Houston
www.mfah.org
Two paintings

McNay Art Museum, San Antonio, Texas
www.mcnayart.org
Two paintings

Cincinnati Art Museum, Cincinnati, Ohio
www.cincinnatiartmuseum.org
Two paintings

Columbus Gallery of Fine Arts, Ohio
Two paintings

(PA Photos)

Wadsworth Atheneum, Hartford
www.wadsworthatheneum.org
Two paintings

Toledo Museum of Art, Ohio
www.toledomuseum.org
Two paintings

Dallas Museum of Art, Dallas, Texas
www.dallasmuseumofart.org
Two paintings

Further museums that hold one work
of art by Cézanne include:
Brooklyn Museum, New York
Chrysler Art Museum, Norfolk, VA
Virginia Museum of Fine Arts,
Richmond
Fine Arts Museums of San Francisco,
San Francisco, California
Smith College Museum of Art,
Northampton, MA

Other countries that house the
works of Cézanne in organizations,
institutions, museums, and
galleries include:

Australia
National Gallery of Victoria,
Melbourne
www.ngv.vic.gov.au

Brazil
Museu de Arte de Sao Paulo Assis
Chateaubriand, Sao Paulo
www.masp.uol.com.br

Canada
National Gallery of Canada, Ottawa
www.gallery.ca/english/

Czech Republic
Národni Galerie, Prague
www.ngprague.cz

Denmark
Ny Carlsberg Glyptokek, Copenhagen
www.glyptoteket.dk

France
Musée d'Orsay, Paris
www.musee-orsay.fr

Germany
Nationalgalerie, Berlin
www.smb.spk-berlin.de

Israel
The Israel Museum, Jerusalem
www.english.imjnet.org

Japan
Yoshii Galerie, Tokyo
www.yoshiigallery.com

Bridgestone Museum of Art, Tokyo
www.bridgestone-museum.gr.jp

Netherlands
Stedelijk Museum, Amsterdam
www.stedelijk.nl

Norway
Nasjonalgalleriet, Oslo
www.nationalmuseum.no

Russia
Pushkin Museum of Fine Arts, Moscow
www.museum.ru

Spain
Thyssen-Bornemisza Collection,
Madrid
www.museothyssen.org/thyssen_ing

Sweden
Nationalmuseum, Stockholm
www.nationalmuseum.se

United Kingdom
National Gallery, London
www.nationalgallery.org.uk

Tate Gallery, (Tate Modern), London
www.tate.org.uk/modern/

Ashmolean Museum, Oxford
www.ashmolean.org

Fitzwilliam Museum, Cambridge
www.fitzmuseum.cam.ac.uk

National Museum of Wales, Cardiff
www.museumwales.ac.uk

Glasgow City Art Gallery
(Burrell Collection)
www.glasgowmuseums.com

National Gallery of
Scotland, Edinburgh
www.nationalgalleries.org

(PA Photos)

■ **ABOVE: Visitors to the Tate Gallery in London.**